MW01231698

Disclaimer:

The information contained in this book is neither intended as tax advice nor advice to those who invest in the financial markets; nor is it intended as promoting or encouraging investment in any specific securities or investments. The author, et al, hereby disclaims any responsibility for any losses suffered by anyone caused by a reliance on the information contained in this book. For any tax advice or investment advice, contact your tax attorney, accountant, or investment counselor.

For Nancy and Dick John
who came to my home
as strangers and have
become dear friends
Have fun reading
this!

Love,
Luciy
February 25, 2013

Money! ... Cool

by

Judith Fabris

Illustrated by Carol Brolin

Archipelago Press
Los Gatos, California

Copyright © 2002 by Judith Fabris

All rights reserved under International and Pan-American Copyright Conventions. Issued under the seal of the Copyright Office. Published in the United States by Archipelago Press
Los Gatos California

Library of Congress Control Number 2003111099

Fabris, Judith 1935-
ISBN 1-893335-12-7
1. money-stock market young investor 2. securities
3. economics 4. stock-bonds 5. mutual funds 6. college savers 7. Wall Street
I. Title

Cover Design by Pro Color

Archipelago Press
Los Gatos, California

Printed in the United States of America

Dedication

To my grandchildren, Alexandra, James, Jordan and Sharif, and to their parents, and to my husband especially, for his unfailing encouragement.

ACKNOWLEDGMENTS

I want to thank all the members of my writing group for their indefatigable support, and also all the children whose enthusiasm for the subject matter made this book a joy to write. Without them, this book would probably never have come to fruition. To my Editor, Crystal Chow, I give my heartfelt appreciation for her excellent comments and guidance. Also, I give much thanks to Kelly J. Felsted for her attention to detail.

Message to the Reader

In 1772, a reddish-haired young man named Alexander Hamilton disembarked from a sailing ship that had carried him from his island home in the West Indies to America. Once he got here, Hamilton rose from poverty and obscurity to become our first Secretary of the Treasury. Today, his picture appears on our ten-dollar bill.

From this book, you will learn the basics of stock market finance and gain an understanding of our country's economic structure that Hamilton so strongly influenced.

To me, the stock market is endlessly fascinating because it is constantly changing and there are always new things to learn. I want to share my enthusiasm for it with you.

The Author

"The potential possibilities of any child are the most intriguing and stimulating in all creation."

Ray L. Wilbur

To Parents, Grandparents and Teachers:

Writing a book to teach children financial concepts has its obvious difficulties. I believe I have resolved these problems by addressing each stock market concept in individual chapters. In this way Money! ... Cool can be read at one time, or the appropriate chapter can be used to augment a specific lesson plan. None of the topics can be covered thoroughly, as it would be well beyond the scope of the age of the children for whom this book is written. The topics covered will help meet your state's math standards for sixth and seventh graders as well as give them an insight into an exciting and adult world of investments.

The extensive glossary will be useful to anyone new to the financial world, whether child or adult.

Table of Contents:

Chapter 1

Julie Carlson stood in the doorway of her brother's room. Her long brown hair was wringing-wet, and so were her denim jeans and pink-flowered shirt.

"What happened to you?" asked Kevin.

"I just finished giving the dog a bath."

"Looks like you're the one who got the bath," her older brother replied.

"I know. I guess I should have worn my bathing suit. Anyway, I'm through with the chores Mom gave me to do today. Are you?"

"Yeah, I finished all of mine this morning. Hey, go get cleaned up and then let's ask Dad if he'll drive us to the mall. There's a new science fiction movie playing. Want to go?"

"Great idea, Kev. Be back in a flash!"

A short time later, Julie and Kevin went downstairs to the family room that their architect dad used as a home office. Sure enough, they found him working at the computer.

"Dad, will you drive us to the movie this afternoon?" asked Kevin.

"What did your mom say about it?" he responded.

"The usual stuff. As long as homework and house chores are done and we use our allowance to pay for the movie, it's okay," said Julie.

"All right, then. Just let me finish this design I'm working on, and then I'll take you. I'm almost done."

This sounds like it might be a typical weekend in any family's household. As Kevin and Julie go off for their weekend afternoon fun, let's review some of the things in their lives that have been mentioned so far. For instance: movies, science fiction, computers, a mall and allowances. Most of these things are so familiar that you might not think of them as significant, but imagine if Kevin and Julie lived 200 years ago. Where would you find them? What do you think their lives would be like?

Unless the Carlson family was extremely wealthy, Kevin would be in the fields using a hoe that his father had forged, or in the barn helping to feed the livestock. Julie would be in the house helping her mother with the washing, cooking and other household chores.

There were no computers or science fiction movies or shopping malls back then. There was no money, either, as we know it. We are accustomed to a nickel in Indiana being the same as a nickel in California or New York or anywhere else in America, but 200 years ago, each of the original 13 states had its own system of *coinage*. The first national coins were minted in Philadelphia in 1792.

When America was a very young country, it had a small population and an abundance of good, cheap land that attracted farmers. Most business was conducted by wealthy farmers or by traveling merchants. *Surplus earnings* from agriculture were usually put back (*reinvested*) into the farm. This is probably what Julie and Kevin's father would have done.

When George Washington became president in 1789, he appointed Alexander Hamilton to be Secretary of the Treasury.

This meant he was responsible for the monetary system of the United States. Hamilton submitted his ideas for a federal bank in 1790. He wanted to establish a *credit system* to pay back the citizens of our young country who had lent money to finance the Revolutionary War.

It was crucial for the government to take steps to pay the *debt* that had resulted from the Revolutionary War. Hamilton thought that if the debt from the war were made the sole responsibility of the federal government, our nation's credit would be restored.

He also believed that if interest rates were lowered, an increase in investments in land and industry would occur. These investments of capital (the use of money and/or property) would multiply, along with jobs and wages.

Interest is what is paid for the use of money. When you borrow money, you pay interest. When you put your money in a savings account, for example, you are actually lending money to the bank. The bank pays you interest for this loan, and if the interest rate is high, you have a good reason for not only keeping your money in a savings account, but adding to it, too.

One of the first truths of our *economic system* is that when interest rates are high, people save more and spend less. When interest rates are low, people save less and spend more.

Write your own definition of the following terms:

Surplus earnings

Coinage

Reinvest

Credit system

Economic system

Debt

Interest

Activities

If possible, visit a U.S. Mint. They are located in Washington D.C., Philadelphia, Denver, San Francisco, New Orleans, Dahlonega, GA, Charlotte, NC, Carlson City, NV, or West Point, NY.

Read a biography of Alexander Hamilton.

Compare the debt of the United States today with that of Hamilton's time. (The total debt from Pre-Revolution to Post-Revolution was $77 million.)

Quiz

1.   Who was Alexander Hamilton?

2.   What do you think was his most important accomplishment? Why?

3.   What are the differences between the lives of colonial Kevin and Julie and that of today's Kevin and Julie?

4.   What period of time would you like to live in? Why?

Chapter 2

Let's say you would like to own a part of Disneyland or Disney World, or the company that makes Barbie and Ken dolls. You can do this by buying *stock* or *shares* of stock.

Shares of stock represent ownership in a particular company. To own a part of Disneyland or Disney World, you would buy shares in the Walt Disney Company. You could also purchase stock in the Mattel Corporation, which is the company that manufactures Barbie and Ken dolls. If you purchased shares of stock in either or both of these companies, you would be what is called a *shareholder.*

Let's suppose Mattel stock is trading for $40 a share. *"Trading"* means the price at which a share can be bought or sold on any given day. It also means that when the stock was last bought or sold, the price was $40 a share. For $40 you could be a shareholder in the Mattel Corporation.

Shares of stock are purchased through companies called *stockbrokerage houses.* They are also known as *securities firms.* The men and women who buy or sell stock on your behalf are called *stockbrokers,* or just brokers. Stock may be purchased in the brokerage office, by telephone or by computer. Trading by computer is very popular today, and is called online trading.

Unfortunately, anyone under the age of 18 is considered a minor and cannot purchase stock on his or her own. A parent or *guardian*, however, can purchase stock for you under what is termed a *custodial account*.

Many adults open custodial accounts at brokerage houses to buy stock for their children or grandchildren. These accounts are used later for college expenses, or for other personal needs.

Every state has its own set of laws regarding custodial accounts under the Uniform Gift to Minors Act. Depending on where you live, your state may use the abbreviation *UGMA* or *UGTMA*.

Today it is possible to buy only a portion of a share of stock. When someone does that, it is called buying a *fraction* of a share, or a fractional share.

As you know from your math studies, one whole number can be divided into several parts, and these parts are called fractions. You probably use fractions every day without even thinking about it. Now, knowing fractions will make it much easier for you to read and understand the *stock market* pages in the newspaper.

The price of a stock could be a whole number like $40 in the Mattel example, but it could also be a number with fractions. Each fraction is expressed in eighths - 1/8, 1/4, 3/8, 1/2 and so forth. This series of fractions represents parts of prices that stock can be sold for. (It is possible for stock to trade in many kinds of fractions, but we will concern ourselves only with the eighths series of fractions for now.)

The following chart shows how one dollar can be divided:

1	1.00	100 cents
⅞	.875	87 ½ cents
¾	.750	75 cents
⅝	.625	62 ½ cents
½	.500	50 cents
⅜	.375	37 ½ cents
¼	.250	25 cents
⅛	.125	12 ½ cents
0	.000	0 cents

You are used to buying things in stores or restaurants and paying the price that is marked on the tag or on the menu. You may not have thought much about it, but usually the price is about the same from one shopping trip to the next. When a price **does** change, it usually goes down. In other words, you may pay less for something because it is a "special" or "sale" price.

Recently, Julie's grandmother went shopping for a birthday present for her. She found a dress in Julie's size that had originally been priced at $34.95, but it was "on sale" for $26.95. The price for things we buy in stores usually stays at the amount that is marked on the tag, but sometimes it is marked down for a sale.

The price of stock, however, can *fluctuate*. That means that it can go up **or** down. If a stock is not popular with the investing public, the price may be lowered, just as the price for Julie's dress was. If the demand for a stock is high, however, the price of the stock will go up.

Write your own definition of the following terms:

Stock

Share

Shareholder

Stockbrokerage house

Securities firm

Stockbroker

Broker

Guardian

Custodial account

Custodian

UGTMA

UGMA

Trading

Stock market

Fraction

Increment

Fluctuate

Activity

As a group, read financial articles from daily
newspaper and discuss them.

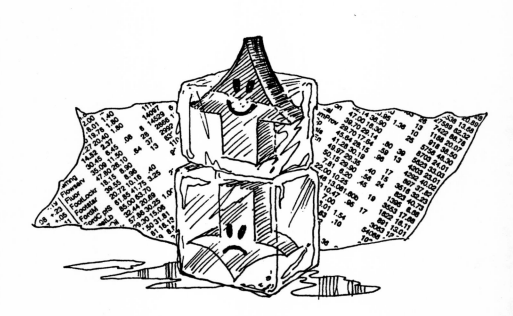

Quiz

1.   Put the following numbers in order, starting with the smallest: 3/4, 3/8, 7/8, 1/8.

2.   Which number is the largest: 40 1/4 or 40.25?

3.   Which number is the smallest: 23 7/8 or 23 1/27?

4.   Show the different ways you can write 3/8.

5.   If you were going to build a tall building, or a house, why do you think fractions might be important?

Chapter 3

One rainy afternoon, Julie and Kevin were visiting with their grandparents. They wandered into the kitchen where Grandma Carlson was baking cookies.

"Where's Grandpa?" Julie asked.

"Well, if I know him, he's got his nose buried in his newspaper in the living room," Mrs. Carlson replied.

Kevin went into the living room and found his grandfather sitting in his big chair by the fireplace, reading *The Wall Street Journal.*

"What's so interesting, Grandpa?" Kevin asked. "That paper doesn't even have the comics in it."

"Come and sit by me. We'll talk about what's in this particular newspaper, and I'll show you how it relates to a new car."

Julie joined her brother and they each sat on an arm of their grandfather's chair where they could peer over his shoulder at the newspaper.

"Let's see. What kind of car does your mom want?" Mr. Carlson asked.

"She told Dad, 'Nothing but a Buick'," Kevin said.

"A Buick, huh? Okay. 'Buick' is the name given to one kind of car that is *manufactured* by General Motors. They also make Chevrolet, Pontiac, Oldsmobile and Cadillac. Each of these kinds of cars are built by a division of General Motors. All of the divisions combined form a *corporation* called General Motors.

"General Motors is also a stock. It trades on the New York Stock Exchange."

"What's the New York Stock Exchange, Grandpa?" asked Julie.

"It is a place in New York City where men and women buy and sell stock for people from all over the country. Many people refer to this part of New York City as 'Wall Street.' Wall Street is considered the financial heartbeat of America."

"Why, Grandpa?"

"Because that is where the stock market began a long time ago. It was named for a wall that kept livestock in and enemies away from New York's first settlement. People used to stand on the side of the street in front of taverns, which today are called restaurants or bars, and trade livestock.

"Now, let's see. We were talking about General Motors, weren't we?" Mr. Carlson continued.

"Yes. Buick parts," Kevin reminded his grandfather.

"That's right. Now, suppose that the company that supplied General Motors with a specific part necessary to manufacture Buicks decided not to make the part anymore. General Motors would be faced with an important decision. They would have to decide whether it would be more *economical* to find another supplier to manufacture the part for them, or build a factory and produce the part themselves. Either solution could take a lot of time and money.

"In the meantime, the price of Buick could rise, especially if a lot of people wanted to buy one like your mom does."

"I'm a little confused, Grandpa," said Kevin.

"Yeah, you lost me, too," Julie said. "I don't see why the price of a Buick would change just because of a small part."

"It's because of something called '*supply and demand*.' "

Just then, Grandma Carlson came in with a tray of chocolate chip cookies still warm from the oven.

"If you want to talk about supply and demand, dear, why not use these cookies as an example?"

"I can relate to that!" exclaimed Kevin.

"Me, too," said Julie.

"That's not a bad idea," Grandpa Carlson said. "Go help your grandmother bring the milk and napkins, and then we'll sit at the dining room table and talk about what supply and demand means."

After everyone was seated, Grandpa Carlson said, "The first thing to do is count the cookies. That tells us our supply."

"There are a dozen on this tray, but there are plenty more where they came from," said Grandma Carlson.

"Well, for now, let's pretend that these are all that we have. Furthermore, let's pretend that we can't make anymore, and that there are none at the store."

"Okay, that means we each have a supply of three cookies," said Kevin.

"Right. Except that Julie is already eating one of hers, so she will soon have only two. Suppose we save ours and Julie eats the two she has left. Later, she comes to you or me or Grandma wanting more cookies. Remember, the three we each have are the only ones left and there are no more to be had. How valuable are they now?"

"Wow!" exclaimed Kevin. "I'll bet she'd give me her whole allowance for them!"

"Do you think you would do that, Julie?" asked her grandmother.

"Well, it's hard to imagine no more cookies, but I see what you mean now about supply and demand.

If there is a low supply of something that somebody really wants, then the value of it goes up," said Julie.

"Exactly right, Julie," said her grandfather. "Now, your grandmother has already told us that there are more in the kitchen. Let's imagine that she made thousands of cookies this afternoon."

They all laughed at the idea of mountains of cookies piled up in their grandmother's kitchen, but soon both Kevin and Julie understood what their grandfather was saying.

"There's no way I could eat that many cookies, no matter how good they are," said Kevin. "What would be left over would get stale, and then I wouldn't want them."

"So, now what do you think would happen if Julie came to you for more cookies?" asked Grandpa Carlson.

"I'd be glad to get rid of them, I guess," said Kevin.

"You can bet I wouldn't give you my whole allowance for them," Julie said.

"So, there it is. When the demand is higher than the supply, the price goes up.

When the supply is higher than the demand, the price goes down."

"Now I see why the price of Buick would go up if General Motors couldn't make as many as before," said Julie.

"Yeah, and that was just because of one small part for the car, not the whole thing like with the cookies," added Kevin.

Kevin and Julie noticed that their grandfather was opening his *Wall Street Journal* to the "Money and Investing" section.

"Grandpa, what is this *Dow Jones* that is mentioned so many times? Is it a person or what?" asked Julie.

"Dow Jones is the name of a very old financial company that established a way to measure how the stock market is doing. It has 30 stocks in it. See?" said Mr. Carlson as he pointed to the paper.

"So, there are only 30 stocks?" asked Kevin.

"No. It's just that the people at Dow Jones decided that these 30 stocks were the most stable of all of the corporations that have *publicly traded* stock. These are all corporations called 'industrials.' See, there's General Motors," answered Mr. Carlson.

"What does 'publicly traded' mean?" asked Julie.

"That means that anyone can buy and sell a particular stock. Notice the three capital letters here," Mr. Carlson said as he continued to explain each column. "These letters stand for the name of the company. It's like a nickname. DIS is short for Disney. General Motors uses the *symbol* GM.

"Now, if I were to call my stockbroker and say that I wanted to buy Disney stock, he or she would give me what is called the '*ask*' *price*. That means I could purchase Disney stock right then at whatever that price is. If I owned Disney stock and wanted to sell it, I would be given the '*bid*' *price* and perhaps the last trade price. That doesn't tell me whether it was a bid or an ask, but it does tell me that someone has bought or sold Disney stock."

Grandpa Carlson pointed to the column showing Disney's last trade of the day at 15 ½.

"This means that the last sale of Disney stock that day occurred at the price of $15.50.

"The dividend of 84 cents means that Disney gives 84 cents to each person who owns stock in its company for each share of stock that he or she has. Dividends are paid to investors quarterly, which means four times a year.

"Investors are people who buy stock, like me or your father and mother. Dividends tell us how much of a *return* we would receive on an investment. Based on the price of the Disney stock, at 15 ½, and a dividend of 21 cents, a quarter of the return on an investment of Disney stock will *yield* 1.35 percent.

"To find the yield or return of any stock that pays a dividend, you must use division. Here, I'll show you."

Mr. Carlson picked up his calculator and divided the amount of the dividend by the price of the stock.

"Now, let's look at this column where it says P/E. That means *price/earnings ratio*. Based on the price of the stock, the ratio of price to earnings is 28.75."

"I don't get it," Julie said.

"It is a way of measuring the *performance* of a company based on its earnings in relation to the price of the stock. Many investors use P/E ratios to determine whether or not it is a good idea to buy a stock at a particular price."

Mr. Carlson got up and walked over to his desk. He sorted through several pieces of paper until he found the one he wanted and brought it back to the dining room table.

"This is called a *Standard & Poor's sheet*," he said, showing it to them. Most of the time, people refer to it as 'S & P.' "

"What's it for?" asked Julie.

"It's so that investors like me can read and learn about companies before deciding to *invest* in them. Reading *S&P* sheets is like studying or doing *research*, which you already know how to do. Bet you didn't know that grown-ups have homework to do, too, did you?"

Julie shook her head and said, "I just thought you were doing something you liked to do."

"I do like to do it, Julie. Believe it or not, just because it's homework doesn't mean it can't be fun," her grandfather replied.

"Where did you get this sheet, Grandpa?" asked Kevin.

"My stockbroker gave me this one, but you can also find them at the library," answered Mr. Carlson.

"Gee," said Julie. "We've really learned a lot today."

"Yeah. It turned out to be fun, after all," said Kevin. "May we do this again next time we come over?"

Mr. Carlson grinned and said, "The financial pages or the cookies?"

Write your own definition of the following terms:

Economical

Manufacture

Supply and demand

The Wall Street Journal

Invest

Dow Jones

Corporation

Publicly traded

Listed

Bid price

Ask price

Last trade

Dividend

Price/earnings ratio

Stock symbol

Standard & Poor's sheet

S&P

Research

Research report

Return

Yield

Activities

Compare the kind of information found in *The Wall Street Journal* with your own city's newspaper. What is different? What is the same?

Visit the business section of your public library. Look at a Standard & Poor's sheet to learn what a company does, the dividend it pays, etc.

Locate other companies *listed* in the Dow Jones index. What are they?

Choose two or three companies and follow them for three days. Find out what each of the companies does by getting a Standard & Poor's sheet on each of them.

Keep track of the closing prices for each company. Are their stock prices going up or down? Is there a fractional gain or loss? How much? What is the dividend for each company?

Calculate what the yield would be on each stock that you are following.

Chapter 4

One of Julie and Kevin's favorite outings is going to a McDonald's for a hamburger, french-fries and a Coke.

McDonald's originated in Illinois, but now its restaurants can be found all over the world. Each location is called a *franchise*, which means it is an individual restaurant owned by someone who pays a fee for the right to use the McDonald's name and sell its food.

Mr. and Mrs. Brody, Julie and Kevin's aunt and uncle, recently started a biscuit-baking business. Mrs. Brody's homemade biscuits taste so good that her family and friends have always told her that they were as delicious as any to be found in stores or restaurants. The Brodys knew that baking biscuits on a *commercial* basis would be much different from baking them just for the family, but they decided to try it.

The Brodys began their new business right in their own kitchen. Mrs. Brody baked biscuits every day and after school, while Kevin and Julie's cousins delivered the biscuits to several restaurants in the town where they live.

Mr. Brody took care of the business details after coming home from his job at the hardware store. The business grew and soon it required more than just the family's spare time. They found that there was a lot of work involved with purchasing baking supplies, billing customers (accounts receivable) and paying suppliers (accounts payable). Mr. Brody eventually left his job at the hardware store to work full-time on their new business.

As time passed, the orders for biscuits increased so greatly that it was impossible for the family to deliver all of the orders themselves. Mr. and Mrs. Brody had to buy delivery trucks and hire people to drive them.

Not long after that, it became necessary to hire more bakers to help Mrs. Brody make biscuits, but the kitchen was too small for all of them to work in at once.

The Brodys realized that they had to raise capital in order to *expand* their business. "*Capital*" is the term for money that is used to make businesses grow. The way businessmen and businesswomen raise capital is by changing their "capital structure," which means how the company is put together.

Mr. and Mrs. Brody went to a bank and presented a business plan showing how they could use the money that they wanted to borrow. They included copies of orders from their customers to show how high the demand was for Mrs. Brody's biscuits.

Their plan was that part of the money would be used to rent a store and install baking equipment, and some of the money would go toward hiring more employees to help Mr. Brody with the paperwork.

Once the bank approved the loan, the Brodys

set about moving the business out of their home and into the rented store.

As a result, the business grew even bigger. The Brodys were successfully handling more and more orders since they had more people and equipment. They knew that if they wanted to continue to expand, it was time to take another step with their rapidly growing business.

This time, the Brodys visited a lawyer. The lawyer turned their biscuit business into a *corporation*. The new company was named Brodys' Batter Biscuits, and soon everyone called it just BBB.

The Brodys moved out of the rented store after a new bakery building was completed. When Mr. Carlson heard that the Brodys' baking business had moved into an even larger location, he called Mr. Brody to see if he could bring Julie and Kevin over.

"It would be great to see all of you, Tom," said Mr. Brody. "I'll be happy to give you a tour, if you'd like."

"We'd really enjoy that, Jim, and maybe while we're there, you could explain a little of what it's been like to start a business," said Mr. Carlson.

As Mr. Brody guided the Carlsons through the large rooms of the new bakery, he explained that they had just incorporated.

"The bank provided us with the financing to build this bakery and we were able to purchase the latest equipment."

"Gosh, Uncle Jim. I didn't know that bakeries were this big," said Kevin. He watched wide-eyed as the bakers pulled large pans of biscuits from several huge ovens.

"Neither did I, in the beginning," Mr. Brody responded. "When your Aunt Jean and I started making biscuits on a commercial scale, we learned a lot of things."

"Like what?" asked Julie.

"Well, for one thing, we had to make studies called 'demographics.' Do you know what demographics are?"

Kevin and Julie shook their heads.

"Demographics are a statistical study of people's habits. The statistics we needed were the number of people in the area who buy ready-made biscuits, as well as how many biscuits they bought over a certain period. We also had to find out what restaurants and fast-food chains have biscuits on their menu.

"Once we had all of this information, we took our findings to our banker to support our need for expansion.

"Your Aunt Jean and I also called on several local restaurants to see if we could get contracts to supply them with biscuits.

"Several of the restaurants agreed to contract with us, but they also wanted us to supply them with bread and rolls, too. That meant we needed to get new recipes and more supplies for mass production. But, that wasn't all.

"We soon discovered that there's more to the baking business than just the quality of the products. Having a bakery required more employees to do the baking, packaging and delivering of our finished products. This is all part of the *operations* end of the business."

"We needed more people to run the office, also. That's where we take orders for our baked goods, bill our customers and pay our bills for supplies. This is the *administrative* part of the business."

"You and Jean sure have come a long way from your kitchen, Jim," said Mr. Carlson.

"I know. And I haven't even begun to tell you about the marketing and advertising that we're involved in," Mr. Brody answered. "But, I think Kevin and Julie have absorbed enough business information for one day. We'll save that subject for another time.

"Now," he continued, "no tour of a bakery is complete without a free sample. Shall we go see if there are any hot biscuits with your names on them?"

Write your own definition of the following terms:

Capital

Commercial

Expand

Corporation

Administrative

Operations

Franchise

Incorporate

Activities

Invite a business owner to tell your class about his or her business and how it grew.

Visit a business in your community and interview the owner about how it works.

Quiz

1.   What kind of financial information do you think a banker might want to know aout Mr. and Mrs. Brody's baking business?

2.   What information do you think you would need to keep track of for a baking business?

3.   Other than financial information, if you were going to lend money to BBB, what would you want to know about the company?

Chapter 5

Julie unwound the bright yellow bow from the colorfully wrapped package. It was the last one of the many presents that surrounded her place at the dining room table. Kevin, her mother and father, and Grandpa and Grandma Carlson watched with great interest.

She tore through the birthday paper to the plain white box. She shook it, but could hear nothing.

"Hurry up, Julie," said Kevin impatiently. "See what else Grandpa and Grandma gave you."

Julie opened the box, but it seemed to be filled with nothing but white tissue paper. Then she found a large white envelope. She opened it and pulled out a piece of paper.

"Read what it says, Julie," said her father.

"Center City, California Water Bond 5 percent due June 15, 2011."

"I don't know what this is," said Julie, puzzled.

"Look at the center of the *bond*, below the picture. See where it says. $5,000?" asked her father.

"Yes," said Julie hesitantly.

"That means that Grandpa gave you money that will be yours in the year 2011. Just in time to help you go to college. In the meantime, you will earn 5 percent *interest* on that $5,000 each year, which equals $250 a year," said her father.

"Wow! That's a lot of money, Dad." She paused.

"Why would the city have a piece of paper that would say all of this stuff?" Julie said thoughtfully.

"Well, Julie, do you remember the new buildings that were built last year in the civic center?" her grandfather asked.

"I do," said Kevin. "Dad was the architect."

"That's right, Kev."

"This paper represents one of those buildings?" asked Julie.

"Well, in a way," her father answered. "The city needed to raise money, or capital, to build those buildings. So, they borrowed the money from people like your grandfather. He lent them $5,000 and became a *creditor*.

"The city then gave him this piece of paper that represents his loan to the city. This bond is evidence that the city owes you $5,000 that will be paid on June

15th in the year 2011. In the meantime, you will earn that interest each year."

"Gosh, Julie. Looks like you own part of a city," said her brother.

Grandpa Carlson smiled. "That's right, Kevin. She's our *'novice tycoon.'* "

Julie thought some more. "Do other cities issue bonds?"

"Oh, yes, Julie. Your gift from Grandpa and Grandma is called a *municipal bond*. Municipal bonds are issued or sold by cities, counties and states. They can also be sold by school districts, parks or hospitals," her mother replied.

"But those are not the only kinds of bonds, Julie," her grandmother said.

"What other kinds are there?"

"Companies or corporations can issue bonds. Our telephone company issues bonds, and so does General Motors. Also, your mother and I have been buying *zero-coupon bonds*."

"What kind of bond is that?" asked Julie.

"That's a type of government bond issued by the federal government, not a municipality," her mother answered.

"We bought them when you very young for $200 or $300 a bond. When the bond matures, we will get back $1,000 per bond. A *maturity* date means the time we will receive back the face amount investment. We plan to use these bonds to help us pay for your college education, so most of them will mature in 15 to 20 years."

"Does Disney sell bonds?"

"Yes, they do," Grandpa Carlson said. "Bring me the newspaper, Kevin, and we will look at the bond pages and see who else we recognize."

"By the way, do you know what happens every April 15th?" asked their dad.

"No," said Julie and Kevin together.

"Mom and I, Grandpa and Grandma, and millions of other Americans pay their income taxes."

"Some kinds of bonds give people income that they must pay taxes on. That type of income is called '*taxable* income'," he continued. "That's the difference between municipal bonds and *corporate bond*s.

"The interest that Julie receives will not be taxable because it is a municipal bond. If it were a bond from a corporation like Disney, the interest would be taxable."

Kevin brought the paper to the table and began looking through the pages.

"Dad, there are all kinds of pages that say bonds."

"I know, Kevin. Sometimes it can be very confusing for any investor because there are so many kinds of bonds."

"Where can we find Julie's bond?"

"You can't find it in the newspaper. Once a municipality or city sells its bonds, you may never see them listed again. And, if they were, it wouldn't be in a newspaper. Bond prices go up and down based upon the current interest rates. If the interest rate stated on the face of the bond is high and the going interest rate in the economy is low, the bond could be sold at a higher price than what you paid for it. That would be called paying a premium. If the interest rate on the face of the bond were low, and the current interest rate was higher, the bond might be sold at a lesser price than what you paid for it.

That's called a discount. Corporate bonds in a company that you might want to own are sometimes bought and sold more readily than municipal bonds. Just remember, if you hold the bond to maturity, you will receive the full face value of the bond, and the interest each year. Otherwise, if you need to sell it sooner, you might sell it for less than you paid for it.

"The prices of municipal bonds currently for sale are in a daily *publication* called the *Blue List of Current Municipal* and *Corporate Offerings*. Generally, it's just called the *Blue List*. It's a large book made of thin blue paper with printing in dark blue ink. It lists municipal bonds that are available for sale all over the country and even from places as far away as Puerto Rico and the Virgin Islands."

"Where do you buy bonds Grandpa? Did you have to go to the city hall to buy my bond?"

"No Julie, I buy my bonds through my stockbroker. Some securities firms only sell bonds or only stocks. Other firms sell both kinds of securities, stocks and bonds. Remember, stock represents equity or ownership in a company and bonds represent a corporation's or government's debt. Most of the time you won't find a *Blue List* in a brokerage firm's office. The *Blue List* is kept on the trading desk where men and women buy and sell the bonds for my stockbroker and for the other brokers in his firm."

Julie exclaimed, "Oh, talking about the color blue reminds me that I want to try on my other present that Grandma and Grandpa gave me. I really like the idea of being a 'novice tycoon,' but I'm glad I don't have to wait until the year 2011 to wear my new blue dress!"

Write your own definition of the following terms:

Bond

Creditor

Interest

Novice

Tycoon

Municipal bond

Corporate bond

Taxable

Nontaxable

Publication

Blue List

Zero-coupon bond

Maturity

Activities

See how many different kinds of bonds you can find in *The Wall Street Journal.*

Find out if the city where you live has outstanding municipal bonds. If your city doesn't have outstanding bonds, your county will.

Write a short report on the bonds that are outstanding. For what purpose were they issued? When do they mature? What is the interest rate?

Chapter 6

"What are you reading, Kevin?" Julie asked.

"A book about Andrew Carnegie. It's for my class book report."

"Who's he?"

"He was one of the richest men in America. A real tycoon. He gave a lot of money to colleges and libraries. He actually made all of it using other people's money."

"How did he do that?"

"He started out by borrowing the money for his passage to America when he was only 13 years old."

"Gee, you're 13, Kevin, and Mom and Dad won't even let you take the train by yourself!"

"I guess life was a lot different 150 years ago, Julie. But listen to this. When Carnegie was 20, he was working for the Pennsylvania Railroad. One day, his boss offered him 10 shares of a stock called Adams Express. The boss had a friend who wanted to sell his shares.

"Carnegie wanted to buy them, but since he didn't have any money, he asked his boss to let him pay for it on a six-month *installment plan*. His boss agreed, so Carnegie went to a *money-lender* and borrowed the first installment at a high rate of *interest*.

"Then he persuaded his mother to take out a second *mortgage* on the family home to help meet the *repayment* schedule.

"Eventually, with the dividends on the stock and his own *salary*, he was able to repay all the money he owed.

"Three years later, he used his first two investments to buy oil stock. So, by the time he was only 28, he had an annual *income* of more than $40,000 from his stock *portfolio*. You know, Julie, owning shares in more than one stock means you have a stock portfolio. That's a lot of money. My teacher says that Carnegie's portfolio would be worth millions, maybe billions, today."

"Kevin, maybe you and I should borrow money from Mom and Dad to buy stock. We could get rich."

At that moment, Mr. Carlson walked into the room and overheard their conversation.

"People do use other people's money to buy stock, but nowadays it's called buying stock on *margin*," he said. "The money-lender is the brokerage house. That's how people buy stock on a so-called installment plan."

"There's still a stock called Adams Express," said Kevin. "I found it in the list of stocks on the New York Stock Exchange."

"We can go to the library and look it up on a Standard & Poor's sheet and find out more about it, if you'd like," said Mr. Carlson. "Standard & Poor's provides research on most of the traded stocks that investors buy and sell today."

"Do they research all the stocks that exist?" asked Julie.

"No, but they do research all of the companies that are on the New York or American Stock Exchange and many of the stocks that trade *over the counter*."

"What's the difference?" Kevin asked.

"Well, an '*exchange*' means that there's an actual place where orders go when someone wants to buy or sell stock. Over the counter stocks are traded electronically by computer or telephone lines.

"Stocks that trade over the counter usually aren't as well known. One of the company

restrictions might be that the stock can only be traded in the state where it was issued.

"Sometimes there are small new companies that issue stock to raise capital. In fact, kids, if you'd like to, we can visit a company that did that. It's the factory near here that manufactures skateboards."

"Gosh, Dad. That sounds like fun. Do you think they'd give us a free sample like Uncle Jim did?"

Julie and her dad rolled their eyes as Kevin laughed at his own joke.

Write your own definition of the following terms:

Installment plan

Money-lender

Repayment

Salary

Interest

Mortgage

Income

Margin

Over the counter

Portfolio

Exchange

Activities

Look for the following stocks on Standard & Poor's sheets:

International Business Machines (IBM)

Toys 'R' Us (TOY)

Apple Computer (AAPL)

Amdahl (AMH)

Chapter 7

"I'm winning!" Julie exclaimed. She and Kevin were playing Monopoly on the living room carpet.

"See, I have most of the money and houses."

"You're just lucky," grumbled Kevin.

"Maybe I'll be a businesswomen, just like Aunt Jean."

"That's quite an ambition, Julie," said her father. "Your Uncle Jim told me yesterday that they're going to expand BBB again. They are planning to *go public*."

"What's that mean, Dad?" she asked.

"Let's arrange to visit them, and you can find out," replied their father.

They found Mr. Brody sitting behind his large desk going through a pile of papers.

"After talking with our lawyer and our banker," he began, "we decided that it was time to become more widely known, and enlarge our company. To do that, we needed more capital. Our lawyer suggested that we contact a large brokerage house to *underwrite* us. So that's what we did.

"We flew to New York to talk with the *underwriting department* of a major *New York Stock Exchange firm*. That's the department that helps private corporations go public. Mr. Grant, who is in charge of the firm's underwriting department, told us that they could put together an underwriting syndicate to issue stock in BBB to raise our needed capital. BBB is going to be a public company.

"After talking with him, we decided that the new shares of stock would be offered at $10 each. That means that this is what the public will pay for a share of BBB.

"Two million shares will be our initial offering. How much capital will that raise, do you think?" their uncle asked Kevin and Julie.

"Two million times 10. That's $20 million!" gasped Julie.

"That's right. Of course, the underwriting firm will take some money, and any firm that helps underwrite BBB will also receive a small portion. Mr. Grant told me that he might ask two or three more firms to help underwrite the offering. But most of the capital will go to BBB," answered their uncle.

Your Aunt Jean will be the *president*, and I'll be the chief operating officer. We'll hire a chief *accountant* who will be the company *treasurer*. We'll also employ a corporate *secretary*. "Your Aunt Jean will appoint someone to be the supervising baker so that she will be free to be the *chief executive officer* and do administrative work and not spend hours in the bakery.

"Perhaps, as the years go by, BBB will increase its product line even further. In order for us to do this, BBB will need to enlarge the size of its *research and development department*. There are always new recipes and more ways to make bakery goods."

"Can Julie and I buy some stock, too?"

"I'll tell you what, Kevin. I'll open custodial accounts for both of you," said their father. "I know Uncle Jim and Aunt Jean will enjoy having you as shareholders, because they've watched the two of you gobble down enough biscuits!"

Write your own definition of the following terms:

Go public

President

Chief operating officer (COO)

Chief executive officer (CEO)

Treasurer

Secretary

Accountant

New York Stock Exchange firm (NYSE)

Research and development department

Underwrite

Underwriting department

Activities

Find a publicly traded company in your area. Interview one of its officers and learn how the company became public.

Look in the business section of your newspaper to see how many articles you can find about COOs and CEOs. What industries do they represent?

Next time you go out, notice the names of the different fast-food restaurants around you. See if you can find out if they are publicly traded companies.

Look at the wrapper on one of your favorite candy bars to find out the manufacturer's name. Go to the reference desk at the public library and ask the librarian to show you how to find out whether that manufacturer is a publicly traded company.

Choose a product and pretend you are company. Write a report on what you would need to do to take your company public.

Chapter 8

Mr. and Mrs. Carlson were sitting in the living room, poring over what looked to Julie like mountains and mountains of papers.

"Mom, Dad," she called. "What are you two doing with all that paper? Are you actually reading it?"

"Yes, we are honey," her mother answered.

"This is my *retirement plan* from my company and we are trying to figure out what to do," her dad said.

"Don't you just retire when you want to? Doesn't the government give you money every month like Grandpa and Grandma get?"

"Whoa, slow down Julie, you are asking some pretty important questions. Let me answer them one at a time.

"Yes, in some respects I guess I could retire anytime I wanted to, but there is a big question added to that. Suppose I were to retire tomorrow. What would we live on?"

"Money from the government. Isn't that right?" said Julie.

"Wrong," her dad replied. "Today, Mom and I have to look at Social Security, (that's what pension money from the government is called) as just a supplement or an extra to what we need each month. So no, it's not practical to retire until I am much older, or much richer, which ever comes first. You see, Julie,

I'm just going to be 40. Your mom is only 38. In order for me to retire and receive the maximum check each month from the government, I need to wait until I am at least 65. With my retirement plan, I can withdraw after age 59 1/2. I'll probably be in my mid-sixties before I do retire, but of course that could change. The only way I could retire now and receive Social Security is if I get injured on my job, and am unable to work."

"Gosh, Dad, I wouldn't want that to happen," said Julie very concerned.

"Well, neither do we Julie," her father replied.

"Your mom and I are deciding what to do regarding my architectural firm, and also with the money I receive from my consulting.

"We need to determine the way in which we can get the most use out of a retirement plan. You see, Julie, once I put that money in a retirement account, then I shouldn't touch it until I'm allowed to take it out, when I reach the eligible age. And mom and I want to have sufficient money so we don't have to ask Kevin and you to support us." He winked at Mrs. Carlson.

"Oh, Dad. You're so funny."

"Why don't you just put that money into a *savings account* at the bank?"

"We could do that, but there are some special tax considerations. You see when I put money into a retirement account, depending on which account I use, the government tells me how much money I can put in. And if I leave that money there until I retire, I don't have to pay taxes on it.

"That's a pretty good reason for having a retirement plan, Dad."

"Do you remember what Grandpa and I were saying about income taxes? Well, if I put this money that I have earned into a retirement account, I won't have to pay taxes on it. If I just put it into a regular savings account, I will earn interest, but I will have to pay taxes on the interest, and taxes on the money I used to start the savings account."

"Well, where do you put the money if not into a bank?" asked Julie.

"I go to my stockbroker to talk about some possible investment ideas."

"How do you choose a stockbroker anyway, Dad?"

"Well, I use the same person that Grandpa does, but that is a super question."

"What's a super question?" asked Kevin as he walked into the living room to join his parents and Julie.

"Julie asked me how to find a stockbroker."

"Well, I'd like to know, too."

"There are lots of good stockbrokers, son, but when you are starting out, it's best to choose a well-known firm. Pick one, and then make an appointment to see the manager. The manager should then select, a broker for you based on what you have told him or her about your *investment goals*."

"What do you mean, Dad?"

"Well, how are you planning to invest your money? Do you want your stocks to pay dividends? Do you want technology companies like Apple or Intel that just grow and put all their *surplus earnings* back into the company? How much money do you have planned for investments now? Will you be adding more money?

"If a broker who hasn't been in the business a long time is suggested to you, it doesn't mean you should want to go someplace else, but a longer time in the business does show how stable the person may be. Now if you have a lot of money, you will usually be directed to a more senior broker, someone who has been with the company several years.

"Most brokers are paid on commission. That means they earn a fee for everything they do for you with regards to trading. The broker can do research for you, keep you up-to-date on investment news, hold your securities for safekeeping, tell you the latest tax laws, watch your investments, and even put you in contact with an investment counselor if you don't want to manage your own money.

"All stockbrokers have to pass certain tests, so they should be able to answer your questions. But if the broker doesn't listen to what you are saying, then you need to find someone else. One of the most important things to remember is that a stockbroker is basically trying to sell you something."

"Dad, that's really interesting, but you do everything by computer. Why do we need a stockbroker?"

"Kevin, you are learning a lot more than I have been giving you credit for. You are so right. With all the modern technology today, and all the incredible changes coming in the future, if you choose a firm that has on-line information, and you decide you like to do everything yourself, then you can do everything on the computer from opening your account, to research, to getting quotes or buying and selling."

"That sounds like more fun than going to an office," Kevin said.

"Well, I like doing it that way. Now, your grandpa, he'd rather sit face to face with someone."

"I think I want to do everything on the computer, and wait till I'm Grandpa's age to go to someone's office."

"Good idea, Kevin. But you will have to wait until you are 18 at least to do any investing by yourself. In the meantime, you can watch what I do."

Write your own definition of the following terms:

Investment goals

Surplus earnings

Savings account

Social Security

Retirement plan

Pension

Activities

Perhaps your teacher can ask a local brokerage office to send someone to your class at school to talk about investing.

Visit a brokerage office in your community.

Watch a news channel that talks about investments.

Chapter 9

Kevin struggled to get through the front door. He was already juggling books that didn't fit in his backpack, when the mail carrier stopped to give him all the family mail. It wasn't a small amount either.

"Mom, can you help me, quick before I drop everything!"

Mrs. Carlson arrived just in time to keep him from dropping everything.

"Thanks, Mom. I wouldn't have liked to drop everything on the floor. These books are heavy. Why did you get so many heavy envelopes in the mail?"

"Well you dad and I ordered a lot of *mutual fund prospectus*es to see what fund we would like to buy."

"You and Dad have never talked to Julie and me about mutual funds. Are they investments?"

"Yes, they are Kevin, and important ones too. I think this would be a good topic for the four of us to discuss, so go do your homework now, and we'll discuss this at dinner. Okay?"

"Sure, Mom, I have a ton of stuff to do."

At dinner, Mrs. Carlson had several thick booklets sitting at her place, and Mr. Carlson also had some at his.

"Looks like we might just be having paper for dinner," joked Kevin. "I'd much rather have that chicken I saw roasting in the oven."

"Tell you what Kevin, I think your mom will serve up the chicken first, and then we will all digest this mutual fund information," laughed Mr. Carlson.

"What is a mutual fund?" asked Julie.

"A mutual fund is a *management company* that pools investors' money. *Pooling* means that they would take my money, and a lot of other people's money, put it all together and invest it. All the money is mixed in one pot, so to speak," he explained.

"Then the management company takes our money and invests it in various stocks and bonds according to what investment goals we have selected. These booklets, called prospectuses, tell us how the management company will invest our money."

"Do you know the other people who are investing in this pool?" Julie asked.

"It's highly unlikely," her mother answered. "We just want to find the company whose investment goals are most like our own. So we look at the prospectuses to determine that."

"What exactly is a prospectus?" Julie asked.

"How do you know the fund is a good one?" asked Kevin.

"A prospectus, really a fact book, will tell us what the fund is about, who is managing the portfolio, and what stocks and bonds are in it. By reading about what is called their performance, we can find out how much money was made by the portfolio managers," said their father.

"We look up their performance on various Internet sites, and also read through several business magazines and mutual fund *rating* services. Brokerage companies will often have information on their websites to tell us how mutual funds are rated," added Mrs. Carlson.

"What do you mean by rated?" Kevin wanted to know.

"Look at it this way, kids. You both get letter grades in school, A, B, C, D and F. Although you'd better not come home with the last two," Mr. Carlson said. "Anyway, that's how mutual funds are graded too. Sometimes you might think that a fund that is rated A in an up market would be the best to buy. But what if the fund only rated an F in performance when the market was down?"

"I don't think that would be the best one to buy," answered Julie. "But suppose there was no fund that was rated an A in both cases? What kind would you buy?"

"Well, Julie, for me, I'd look for something that was a B in the up market and a B in the down market. That way it would be more consistent," said her mother. "And even if I didn't make the most money, I'd be doing just fine."

"Besides, no one can predict how the market will behave. Everyone has his or her own theory. I just try to find something that has grown consistently over a number of years," Mr. Carlson added. "And that means whether the market was up or down."

"How many funds are there to choose from?" asked Kevin.

"There are absolutely thousands, and more new ones each day," said Mr. Carlson.

"Why don't you buy a brand-new fund then?" asked Kevin.

"Sometimes I would, but then the people managing the fund would have to be known to me as a successful management group," was his reply.

"You kids are so smart about your money questions, I'm going to explain to you about the different kinds of mutual funds.

"Basically, there are two kinds of mutual funds: closed-end and open-end. As a general rule, I wouldn't be buying a *closed-end fund* because they trade on the exchanges just like a stock. That means my money is tied to whether the 'stock' is going up or going down. There are only a set number of shares, and it is rare if the number of shares increase. So a closed-end fund is like the supply and demand theory. If only a few shares of the closed-end fund are available and the demand is high, the price would go up. Of course, if there was no demand, and there was a lot of the fund around, the price would go down.

"An *open-end fund*," Mr. Carlson continued, "on the other hand continuously offers new shares to the investing public, and will redeem the shares if you want to get your money back."

"Now, we can go to a stockbroker to buy some of these funds, but with others we need to go to the company themselves," said Mrs. Carlson.

"How come Mom?" Kevin and Julie asked almost in unison.

"A stockbroker can only sell you the funds that the brokerage house has dealer agreements with. A *dealer agreement* is between the brokerage house and the mutual fund management company, giving the brokerage firm the right to sell the mutual fund to its clients.

"Some fund companies have their own sales force within the company. That's called a *captive sales force*. The people are employees of the mutual fund company and their company's funds are the only ones they can sell."

"Do you mean mutual fund companies have more than one fund?" asked Kevin.

"Oh yes," Mrs. Carlson answered, "What the management company has is a family of funds, all of them with different kinds of investment goals and ways they will invest our money."

"When you buy a closed-end fund, you pay a brokerage commission. When you buy an open-end fund, you may pay a *sales charge*, or you may pay nothing," said Mr. Carlson. "Open-end funds can either be a load or fee kind, or a no-load, no-fee kind," he continued.

"Why would you pay money to buy a fund if you could get another one without paying a fee?" asked Kevin.

"Well, Kevin, answer me this," said Mr. Carlson. "If you could buy a basketball that was owned by Michael Jordan or one that had been owned by your school coach, and you collected basketballs, which one would you buy?"

"That's easy, Dad, I'd buy the Michael Jordan. It might cost me more now, but it would really be worth something in the future."

"You've got the concept down pat, Kev," his father replied. "If the performance and all things about the fund costs a fee, but is so much better than one that doesn't have a fee attached, your mom and I would be better off paying to buy a better fund."

"Why do you buy a fund anyway, Dad?" asked Julie. "Because, honey, your dad and I don't have to watch it every day," her mom replied. "When we buy

a mutual fund, we put our money in and if we can add to it, we do it on a consistent basis. Sometimes the price may be up, sometimes it may be down. But after about five years, we should really see our money grow, if we have chosen wisely."

"If we do this adding regularly, we are doing what is called *dollar-cost averaging*," added her father.

Your father and I have been talking about investing in an *index fund*," said Mrs. Carlson.

"What's that, mom?" asked Julie.

"It's a mutual fund that buys the same securities proportionately to those in a market index," said her father. "Remember when we talked about the Dow Jones? That's an index. Standard and Poors has an index too, called the Standard and Poors 500. It tracks the total return of 500 of the largest public company stocks in the United States. It has 400 industrial stocks. You can see it has a lot more than the Dow does. Besides the industrial stocks, it has 40 utility, 40 financial and 20 transportation stocks."

"What's a utility stock?" asked Kevin.

"The kind of company that supplies us with electricity or gas for our kitchen."

"Oh, I see," said Kevin. "Financial companies are like banks and transportation, railroads and such."

"Kevin, you are just becoming so smart," his father said "But going back to an index fund, your mom and I probably will buy a fund that is actively managed and focuses on the fundamental qualities, rather than an indexed total return.

"Index funds are considered a passive approach

to investing, meaning different standards are used when buying and selling in an index fund. An index fund buys and sells the same securities that are in the index they intend to mirror, like the Standard and Poors 500. In an actively managed fund, the portfolio manager will lock in or keep the gains, and reinvest them in other investments."

"Are there many kinds of index funds?" asked Julie.

"Oh my, yes," said Mrs. Carlson. "I even heard about one that invests in stock-car stocks."

"That's weird," said Julie.

"Gosh, could Julie and I buy a mutual fund with some of the money in our savings accounts?" Kevin asked.

"I actually think that would be a wonderful idea, Kevin," said Mrs. Carlson. "We will go and draw out some money tomorrow."

"And when we go out to Grandpa and Grandma's this weekend, we will look at some of the prospectuses together," said Mr. Carlson. "That way we can all make some thoughtful investment choices."

"I hope Grandma has more chocolate chip cookies waiting for us," Julie answered.

Write your own definition of the following terms:

Prospectus

Mutual fund

Pooling

Management company

Performance

Rating

Open-end fund

Closed-end fund

Dealer agreement

Captive sales force

Sales charge

Dollar-cost averaging

Index fund

Activities

Go to a brokerage house and ask for a mutual fund prospectus. Look at all the different sections so you will know about each one.

Go to the reference desk of your library and ask the librarian where to find a list of mutual fund ratings.

Chapter 10

During the summer, the Carlson's took Kevin and Julie on a trip to New York City. They had a lot of fun staying in a hotel, going to museums and to the zoo. On one of the last days there, their father told them he had another exciting place to show them.

Outside of the hotel, their father hailed a taxi, and off they went through the busy streets to what their grandfather liked to call the "financial heartbeat of America, the New York Stock Exchange."

Inside the stock exchange, Julie and Kevin watched wide-eyed through the glass window. People were waving their hands and running back and forth like mice in a maze. Lights flashed, and letters and numbers changed faster than their eyes could follow.

"This is quite different from the days of trading stock under the Buttonwood Tree," their father said.

"Buttonwood Tree?" asked Kevin with a puzzled face.

"Would you like me to tell you about it?" asked their father.

"Oh, yes," said Julie.

"When America was a young colony fighting for freedom in 1776 France lent us $10 million, redeemable in tobacco. That meant we could pay them back with tobacco rather than money. Do you remember reading about Alexander Hamilton?"

Kevin and Julie nodded.

"Well, when Hamilton convinced Congress to redeem our war debt with an issue of bonds, those bonds were first traded with other commodities like livestock, tobacco and grain.

"This activity soon led a group of 24 men who specialized in trading stock to call themselves brokers.

"They began to meet regularly under a buttonwood tree on Wall Street. The *Buttonwood Agreement*, signed in 1792, called for trading stocks for customers. The brokers agreed to do it at a profit of not less than one-quarter percent. Each broker was also required to give preference to the other brokers.

"The brokers moved indoors in 1793. They met in an upstairs room in a tavern where they could comfortably seat themselves.

"They had membership dues just like your mom and I pay for you to belong to the 'Y.' Instead of calling it memberships though, they used the term '*seats.*' Today, people still buy seats on the New York Stock Exchange."

"Dad, why are the people making those motions with their hands?" asked Kevin.

"You've been to an *auction* before with your mother, haven't you? Did you notice people raising their hands from time to time when the auctioneer would ask for a bid? Well, this is very similar. Each wave that you see the people making is a signal that represents the price being bid or asked for the stock. Signals can also represent the number of shares and the end of a transaction."

"They go so fast. Don't they get mixed up and make mistakes?" asked Julie.

"Well, not usually, because they're pretty good at it, but hand signals eventually will be phased out. Someday, computers will take their place," their father replied.

"They must auction off a lot more stock today than they did in the old days," said Julie.

"Yes," their dad answered, "but today it would be called a continuous market. That's because people are continuing to buy and sell 'trade' during the hours that the stock exchange is in session."

Write your own definition of the following terms:

Auction

Seat

Buttonwood Agreement

Activities

If there is a stock exchange in your city, make arrangements to visit it. They probably have special educational tours.

Special shareholder tours are generally available at companies that are publicly traded. Visit one of these if you can.

Study the history of the New York Stock Exchange.

Write to the New York Stock Exchange and ask for their educational package. (There may be a small fee.)

As a group, conduct an auction in class.

Chapter 11

"I want to talk with you about something very important," said Mrs. Burleigh, Kevin's teacher. She was speaking to his class.

"We've been talking about the stock market while you have been learning math concepts. I do hope that all of you have been discussing what you have been learning with your parents. I know you are still very young, but college is just a few years away. You not only have to be academically prepared but the costs can be phenomenal, too, especially if you want to attend a private college. You're all smart, and might be eligible for scholarships or grants. However, college can be a financial drain on your family if you don't qualify for aid."

"How many of you have a computer at home?" Mrs. Burleigh asked. Most of Kevin's classmates raised their hands. "Wonderful," she replied. "As your homework assignment for this evening, I want you to go look at "savingforcollege.com" You and your parents will learn a lot of valuable information at the web site.

"We've discussed custodial accounts that can have some tax advantages for your parents. But there is something unique about college savers. It's called a *529 plan*. It's been so popular that the custodial account might disappear altogether."

"Why is that?" Kevin asked.

"Because a 529 plan will give your parents a better tax break."

"What's a 529 plan?" Kevin's friend asked.

"Good question, Bobby," Mrs. Burleigh answered. "It's a section of the Internal Revenue Code (tax law) that deals with savings plans for college. What makes a college savings plan different from a custodial account is that a custodial account is considered your asset and it may penalize your parents if they get financial aid for your tuition."

"*State-sponsored* college savings plans make the earnings inside the plan tax-free. It may make a big difference with the amount of taxes that your parents pay. Your parents, or any relative can open an account with as little as $25 or $50 and anyone can add to it. You could, your aunts and uncles could, even your neighbor down the street would be allowed to add money. The money may be used for what are called qualified college costs. That would include your tuition, room and board, books and transportation."

"Does every state have a plan?" asked Kevin.

"Almost every state," answered Mrs. Burleigh. "But everyone is eligible to have a plan, whether it's through the state or a private company."

"I can't wait to get home and talk to Mom and Dad about this," Kevin said as he left school for the day.

"Mom, Dad, Julie, I learned something really interesting in school today," Kevin announced as soon as he got home. "Can I tell you about it now?"

"Of course, Kevin. Let's all go sit in the family room," his father replied.

"Okay son, shoot."

"Mrs. Burleigh was telling us today about saving money for college. She talked about something called a 529 plan. She said it's better than a custodial account. Maybe we can use the money Julie and I are taking out of savings to do this instead. She said you were really going to like it, Dad, especially since everything inside the plan would be tax free. And any money earned inside the plan would be taken out tax-free too. Plus, if I have finished college, and Julie hasn't, the money could be used for her without any taxes, just as if I were continuing to use the money.

"Mrs. Burleigh told us to look at savingforcollege.com on the Internet." "Kevin, your mom and I beat you," his dad laughed. "We just happened to look at that site this morning. Then I called a company your Uncle Jim told me about an *Annuity* Association-College Retirement Equity Fund."

"Wow! That's a long name," said Julie.

"People usually refer to it as TIAA-CREF; it's not such a big mouthful that way," her dad replied. "This is a huge company that parents can make an investment into, similar to a mutual fund. Where we live will dictate what investment choices we can use. One thing made quite clear, however, is that this was an investment, not a guaranteed return of money when you are ready to go to college. It could be a lot, or it could be a little."

"Oh, I understand, Dad. It's just like as if we would buy stock. If it goes up we will have a profit, and if it goes way down, we could lose," said Kevin.

"You're right on, Kev, but some states do have guaranteed accounts."

"But what does that mean, Dad?" asked Julie.

"Honey, it means that whatever money is invested in a program backed by the state, the investor will be guaranteed a certain amount at the time you are ready for school," said her mother.

"So, maybe some of my friends would be better off in a guaranteed account if their parents don't have experience with investments," said Kevin.

"That's very true, Kevin. A family' s circumstances and objectives have to be taken into consideration. The plan that is best for us might not be the best for your friend Bobby."

"Can we put in as much money as we want?" asked Julie.

"Well, states do have limits, but I am quite certain, we won't ever be troubled with that. Besides, each state has its own set of tax benefits."

"How can we open an account, Dad?" asked Julie and Kevin in unison.

"Each account would be set up based on your age. That is, if we open two accounts," said his father.

"Maybe Grandpa and Grandma would like to do it," said Julie.

"The accounts would be in our own names, but we couldn't touch them," said Kevin. "I guess I wouldn't want to until I was ready to go to college. And then we could take out what we needed for books, tuition, and our room and board."

"Kev, with your telling Mom and Dad you want to go to a big university, you'll have to put in your allowance each month, too. Maybe we can save enough so I can go study in Europe. I'd like that," Julie said.

"We'll just have to wait and see about that," her parents said.

Write your own definition of the following terms:

529 plan

State-sponsored

State-guaranteed

Annuity

Activities

Go to *savingforcollege.com* on the Internet and look up information regarding your state.

Chapter 12

Julie was helping her mother fix dinner one evening while her father was working at the computer in the kitchen alcove.

"I've been amazed by all the financial information Julie and Kevin have learned over the past few weeks," her mother commented.

As she spoke, Kevin came through the kitchen door dribbling his basketball.

"It's really not that hard to understand, Mom, after Dad and Grandpa explained some things," he said. "In fact, it's been like learning a game."

"Comparing finance to learning a game is pretty accurate," said his father. "There are rules to follow, but those rules are not as hard and fast as you might find in professional basketball. Just as in a game, it takes some gut reactions."

"What do you mean, Dad?" asked Julie.

"Well, in basketball you use your knowledge and past experience to anticipate how the other players will move. Sometimes, though, your intuition, or gut reaction, dictates what you will do more than your knowledge or experience will.

"For instance, if you were looking for an industry to invest in, you would research the companies in that industry to help you decide which would be a better investment than another. Even with knowledge and experience, though, you might still rely on your intuition."

"I get it," said Julie. "Like, maybe Christmas is a better time to buy into a toy company like Mattel, instead of a car company like General Motors."

"Good thinking, but remember that what the market is doing now shows what our economy will be like in about six months," her father answered.

"So, maybe buy into a toy company in the spring or early summer and not wait until Christmas?" asked Kevin.

"That might be more like it."

"The stock market is more like a puzzle rather than a game for me," said Julie. "I like figuring out what company symbols stand for, and keeping track of stock prices."

"You know, when I see buildings and parks, now, I wonder if the city uses bonds to finance them, instead of just wondering how they were built or designed," said Kevin.

"It sounds as if studying the stock market has opened up a whole new way of looking at the world for both of you," said their mother as she brought the food to the table. "We're very proud of you. You both really have learned that Money is Cool."

Activities

When you have defined all of the terms from the previous chapters, compare your definitions with the ones in the glossary at the back of this book. Once you have learned all of them, you will have increased your vocabulary by more than 100 financial terms and concepts.

Whenever you travel, whether it be on a vacation, or just a quick trip to the grocery store, think about how what you purchase affects our country's economy. Almost everything we eat, for example, from fast food to Thanksgiving dinner, is related to our financial well-being. This is also true of the clothes we wear, the gasoline in our cars and the appliances in our homes.

Write a report on what you have learned from this book and how you can apply this knowledge to your own life. How do you think this knowledge can help you.

Glossary

Accountant:	A person who is the professional keeper of financial records for a business.
Administration:	The managing of people to carry out duties.
Advertise:	To call the public's attention to things for sale.
Agriculture:	The science and art of farming.
AMEX:	The American Stock Exchange.
Annual Report:	Material issued yearly by a company to let shareholders know what the company is doing.
Annuity:	Type of investment.
Ask price:	The lowest price of a security acceptable to a seller at a particular time. Used with a bid price, it is referred to as a quote or quotation.

Assets: All forms of property, real and personal, owned by a person or business.

Auction (auction market):   System of trading stocks through agents or brokers on an organized exchange (NYSE, AMEX).

Bid price: The highest price for a security that a prospective buyer is prepared to pay at a particular time; often referred to as a quote or quotation.

Blue List: A publication on blue paper with blue ink that is published by Standard & Poor's Corporation. It lists municipal bonds that are for sale by various securities firms.

Bond: The debt of a corporation, government or municipality.

Broker: A person who works in a securities firm who can sell stocks and bonds.

Brokerage house: The office of a securities firm through which investors buy stocks and bonds.

Buttonwood Agreement: An agreement made by the original 24 men who were traders of stock on Wall Street. It was the "bare bones" beginning of the NYSE.

Capital: Money or property owned or used in business by a person or corporation.

Capital appreciation: An increase of cash or cash equivalent. It is considered to be "only on paper" unless the investment is sold at a profit. Then it is "realized."

Capital structure: How a company is put together.

Capitalization: The total capital funds of a corporation, represented by stocks, bonds, etc. The stated value of authorized stock of a corporation.

Captive sales force: Salespeople who sell only the product or products of the company they work for.

Chief executive officer: The person who heads all operations of a business.

Closed-end fund: Mutual fund that trades like stock, and has a specific number of shares outstanding.

Coinage: The process of making coins.

Collateral: Anything like stocks or bonds that guarantees payment of a financial agreement.

Commercial: Made or done primarily for sale or profit.

Commodity: Any useful thing; anything bought and sold.

Concept: An idea.

Continuous market: Buying and selling without interruption.

Corporate bond: A bond issued by a corporation rather than a government entity.

Corporation: A legally formed association, separate and distinct from the people who own it.

Correspondence: Communication by exchange of letters, fax, or e-mail.

Creditor: One who has lent money to a corporation and has a bond as evidence of that corporation's debt.

Credit system: The financial method in the world for allowing people to buy and sell, and use checks and currency.

Custodial account: An account with a banking institution or brokerage house, held to benefit a minor.

Custodian: One who guards, watches over or maintains property or records of a minor.

Debenture: A bond that is backed by the general credit of the issuer, not based upon assets owned.

Debt: Something owed by one person to another or others.

Demographics: The science of vital statistics.

Dividend: A share of profits distributed to a stockholder.

Dollar-cost averaging: System of buying securities with fixed dollar amount,

Dow Jones,
Dow, DJ:

An index established by Dow Jones & Company. It is the oldest and most widely quoted of all market indicators. The index refers to the measurement of the rise and fall of the stock market computed by averaging 30 industrial companies listed on the NYSE. It reflects the average of current stock prices.

Economic system:

The system used for the production, distribution and consumption of goods and services.

Economical:

Careful use of what you have at regular intervals.

Economics:

A social science. It concerns the economic system and also has to do with money matters or investments.

Equity:

What you own. Your part of ownership in a corporation.

Exchange:

A place where business is carried out by brokers.

Expand:

To increase the size of something.

Expansion: Increasing in size.

Federal bank: The central bank for a political subdivision. For example, the bank for the United States of America, known as the Federal Reserve.

529 plan: College savings plan named for a section of the IRS code.

Fluctuate: To move up or down; rise or fall.

Fraction: Any number expressed as a ratio.

Franchise: The right to market a product in a particular area. Companies (franchisers) charge a fee for issuing a franchise.

Funding: Pledging a certain portion of revenue to pay for the principal and interest on a debt.

Goal: The end toward which your effort has been directed.

Going public: The first time a company issues stock.

Government bond: The debt obligation of the United States government.

Income: A gain measured in money that comes from capital or labor.

Incorporate: To legally become a corporation. This legality is granted by the state where corporation papers are filed. The corporation issues corporate stock and has corporate officers to run its business.

Index fund: A mutual fund that buys the same securities proportionately to those in a market index.

Indicative: Representing a specific act.

Installment plan: Method of paying a debt with partial payments, usually monthly.

Interest: The cost of borrowing money. The payment an investor receives from a bank (or an investment) for lending his or her money.

Invest: To commit money in order to earn a financial return.

Investing: The act of purchasing an investment.

Investment: A form of security or collectible
                          one acquires for an expected
                          increase in value.

Investment goals: What you want to achieve in
                          the future based on your current
                          investing.

Last trade: The final buy or sell of the stock
                          market day.

Listed (security):   A stock or bond that trades on
                          an organized exchange.

**Management
Company:**   The entity that is responsible for
                          the administrative workings of a
                          mutual fund.

Manufacture: To make a product by hand or
                          machinery.

Margin: The money borrowed from a
                          brokerage house to purchase
                          stocks or bonds. The investor
                          puts up a portion of the money
                          and the brokerage house lends
                          the investor the other portion.

Marketing: A method of enticing the public
                          to buy or sell. Advertising is a
                          method of marketing.

Maturity: The date that the principal on an outstanding bond becomes due and payable to the bondholder.

Money-lender: One who lends money to someone for a stated amount of interest.

Mortgage: The pledging of property to a creditor as security for the payment of a debt.

Municipal bond: A debt security issued by a city, state, municipality or one of its agencies. The principal and interest are repaid through taxes or assessment.

Mutual fund: An investment company that uses the proceeds from the public sale of its shares to invest in various securities for the benefit of its public shareholders.

NASDAQ: National Association of Security Dealers Automated Quote. It is a computerized system with price quotations for stocks that trade over the counter.

Nontaxable: A security that does not have money or duty levied against it. The investor will receive interest without being taxed.

Novice: A person new to a particular occupation or activity; a beginner.

NYSE: New York Stock Exchange.

NYSE firm: A securities firm that has a seat on the New York Stock Exchange.

Operations: The daily workings of a company.

OTC (over the counter): The market where securities not listed on organized exchanges are traded.

P/E ratio Price earnings ratio: The price of a share of stock divided by its earnings per share for a 12-month period.

Pension: The amount of financial resources set aside to provide income benefits at a future date, usually upon retirement.

Performance: How well your investment acts in the market.

Pooling: An accumulation of money combined for investment purposes.

Portfolio: A group of securities held by an individual.

Profit: A gain on a transaction. Returns less expenses.

Prospectus: Publication of company data by a corporation, to describe securities to be offered for sale and conditions of sale.

Publication: Something published that is shown to anyone.

Publicly traded: Stock that trades in an open market that is available to anyone.

Rating: Estimate of the credit standing and business responsibility of person or firm.

Redeem: The act of repurchasing a security by the issuing entity.

Reinvest: To put dividends back into the same investment from which the dividends were paid.

Repayment: The act of paying back.

Research: Careful and systematic study in some particular field of knowledge undertaken to establish facts.

Research report: An article or study of a particular company or companies in one area of business.

Research and Development dept: That part of a company that studies and discovers new products as well as methods to improve existing products.

Retirement plan: A method designed for you to be able to receive money after you stop working.

Salary: The money someone earns at specific intervals in return for working a period of time.

Sales charge: The cost involved in buying a mutual fund.

Savings account: Also known as a passbook account offered by a bank, savings and loan or credit union, which pays interest.

Seat: Membership on a securities
exchange.

Secretary: The person who keeps the
records of share ownership and
meetings of stockholders and
directors.

Securities firm: The name for the business
through which you buy or sell
stocks and bonds.

Security: Another name for a stock or
bond. An investment.

Share: The portion of a company
or business belonging to one
person, represented by a piece
of paper called a certificate.

Shareholder: A person who owns a share, or
shares, of stock in a company.

Short sale: A securities trading technique
for selling stock you do not own,
done when you believe the stock
will drop in price and you can
buy it back at a cheaper price.

Social Security: Pension provided by the
government.

Speculation: Taking a risk in anticipation of a gain on an investment.

Standard & Poor's: A widely used indicator of stock market trends. It is also the name of a company that provides financial information about publicly traded companies.

State-guaranteed: Program secured by state government asset.

State-sponsored: Program authorized by state government.

Stock: Represents ownership in a company.

Stock certificate: A document that is evidence of ownership in a company.

Stock market: A place where stock is traded.

Stock symbol: A short-cut method of describing a stock. Various letters in a particular sequence represent the full company name. For example, GM represents General Motors, and DIS represents Disney.

Stockbroker: A person who works in a securities firm who can sell stocks or bonds.

Supply and demand: An economic term to describe the wants of the population and the amount available to them.

Surplus earnings: The net profit from a company's sales and revenues kept to accumulate after dividends and expenses are paid.

Tariff: The Duty (tax) imposed by a government on imported or exported goods.

Tax: A money charge imposed by an authority on people or property for public purposes.

Taxable income: The amount of income subject to federal income tax. Gross income less adjustments and allowable deductions.

Trading: The process of buying and selling stocks, bonds and other types of securities.

Transaction: A business deal. In the stock market, a buy or a sell of a security.

Treasurer: A financial officer of a company.

Tycoon: A wealthy and powerful industrialist or financier.

UGMA, UGTMA: Uniform Gift to Minors Act.

Underwrite: An agreement to purchase all of a new security for public distribution.

Underwriter: The securities company responsible for the original distribution of a stock that a company wants to issue to the public.

Underwriting department: That part of a securities firm that is responsible for distribution of new stock to the public.

Yield: For stock, the percentage return based on the stated dividend and the current market price of the security. For bonds, the percentage rate of interest divided by the purchase price. Either of these may also be called current yield.

Zero-coupon bonds:　　Debt obligations that the Internal Revenue Service has designated as beneficial for retirement plans or custodial accounts.

Bibliography

Leveler, George L., and Loring C. Farwell, *The Stock Market,* 3d ed., New York; The Ronald Press Co., 1963.

Linton, Calvin D., ed. The Bicentennial Almanac; *200 Years of America 1776-1976.* Nashville, TN: Nelson, 1975.

Magill, Frank N. *Great Events from History:* American Series. Englewood Cliffs, NJ: Salem Press, 1975.

Mayer, Martin. *Wall Street: Men and Money.* New York: Collier Books, 1955.

Sharp, Robert M. *The Lord and Legends of Wall Street.* Homewood, IL: Irwin, 1989.

Sobel, Robert. *The Big Board; A History of the New York Stock Market.* New York: Free Press, 1965.

Wurman et al. *The Wall Street Journal Guide to Understanding Money and Markets.* New York: Simon & Schuster, 1990.

HELPFUL HINTS TO PARENTS, GRANDPARENTS AND TEACHERS

Where you reside is going to determine the types of activities you can arrange for the children. Naturally, a more urban area will offer more choices. Below are the answers to the questions asked at the end of the chapters. Obviously, the answers are not complete. They are just suggestions as to how to start the conversation rolling between you and the children.

SYLLABUS

CHAPTER 1

1. Alexander Hamilton was the first Secretary of the Treasury.

2. He established a centralized banking system that made it possible for each state to trade with each other in the same currency.

3. Modern conveniences such as phones, computers, electricity.

CHAPTER 2

1. ⅛, ⅜, ¾, ⅞

2. The same

3. 23 ½

4. .375, 37 ½ cents

5. To make perfect measurements, so the walls will fit or the door will fit in the wall.

CHAPTER 4

1. Accounting methods, inventory control, debits.

2. Computerized accounting system to track inventory, sales, returns, rent, machinery depreciation, cost of goods.

3. It is making money.

About the Author

Judith G. Fabris began her career on Wall Street in the early sixties. She holds both a business and law degree. Her first published article, "How to Avoid Being a Widow Without Assets", appeared in the New York Stock Exchange Magazine.

Under the name Rhoades, she is the co-author of two books on finance, "The Women's Financial Survival Handbook" and "The Women's Investment Handbook", each published by New American Library.

Through the California Community College system, she obtained a lifetime teaching credential, teaching numerous classes on finance and the stock market, Nationally, she has been a guest lecturer to financial professionals as well as private investors.

In the early nineties, she switched her focus, and worked with several local school districts to establish and teach finance and the stock market as an enhancement to the math curriculum.

Now retired, Judith G. Fabris wrote this book, "Money! ... Cool" especially to appeal to her grandchildren whose ages range from 7 to 13.

About the Illustrator

Carol Brolin grew up in the San Francisco Bay area and completed her undergraduate work at California College of Arts and Crafts in Oakland. She did her graduate work at Parsons School of Design in New York City. Formerly a fashion illustrator for several large department stores, Carol Brolin has also been a community college instructor, teaching fashion illustration/advertising. She loves to do fine painting. Money! ... Cool is her first assignment as a book illustrator.

NOTES:

NOTES:

NOTES:

NOTES:

NOTES:

NOTES:

NOTES:

NOTES:

If you would like to contact the author, please email Judith Fabris at the following:

jfabris@moneycool.biz

Printed in the United States
1379300006B/106-510

9 781893 335127